GREAT MINDS OF SCIENCE

Alexander Fleming

The Man Who Discovered Penicillin

Salvatore Tocci

Enslow Publishers, Inc.

40 Industrial Road   PO Box 38
Box 398   Aldershot
Berkeley Heights, NJ 07922   Hants GU12 6BP
USA   UK

http://www.enslow.com

Library of Congress Cataloging-in-Publication Data

Tocci, Salvatore.
    Alexander Fleming : the man who discovered penicillin / Salvatore
Tocci.
        p. cm.—(Great minds of science)
    Includes bibliographical references and index.
    Summary: A biography of Alexander Fleming, the discoverer of penicillin.

    ISBN-10: 0-7660-1998-5
    1. Fleming, Alexander, 1881–1955—Juvenile literature.   2.
Penicillin—History—Juvenile literature.   3. Bacteriologists—Great
Britain—Biography—Juvenile literature.   [1. Fleming, Alexander,
1881–1955.   2. Scientists.   3. Penicillin—History.]   I. Title.   II.
Series.
    QR31.F5 T63 2002
    616'.014'092—dc21
                                            2001003072
ISBN-13: 978-0-7660-1998-0

Printed in the United States of America

10 9 8 7 6 5

To Our Readers:
We have done our best to make sure all Internet addresses in this book were
active and appropriate when we went to press. However, the author and the
publisher have no control over and assume no liability for the material available on those Internet sites or on other Web sites they may link to. Any
comments or suggestions can be sent by e-mail to comments@enslow.com or
to the address on the back cover.

Illustration Credits: Corel Corporation, p. 20; Library of Congress, pp. 11,
13, 63, 85, 87, 108; Medical Society of the District of Columbia, pp. 26, 28, 33,
38, 44, 51, 55, 71, 77, 89, 93, 105; National Archives, pp. 60, 98; The New
York Post, p. 9; Pressens Bild, p. 100

Cover Illustration: Corel Corporation (background); Medical Society of the
District of Columbia (inset).

Contents

The First
Patients

ALBERT ALEXANDER WAS NOT WORRIED about the scratch on his face. After all, it was just a small scratch from a rose thorn. He felt the cut would heal by itself. But several days after getting the scratch, Alexander developed sores on his mouth. His face became swollen and he developed a high fever. His small scratch had become infected. This infection quickly spread to his scalp and eyes.

Alexander was rushed to a hospital in London, England, where he worked as a policeman. Doctors started giving him large doses of a drug to fight the infection.

Unfortunately, the drug did not work. His lungs and shoulders also became infected.

Two months had passed since Alexander had scratched his face. Doctors now felt that he had only days to live. As a last hope, they decided to try a different drug. However, there was one big problem. The drug had been tested on mice, but it had never been used with humans. This new drug had worked well getting rid of infections in mice. Hoping that it would work as well in humans, the doctors decided to inject Alexander with it. This was followed by more injections, one every three hours. Alexander became the first patient in history to be treated with this new drug.[1]

Within twenty-four hours, the results were amazing. Alexander's temperature returned to normal. He also regained his appetite. Five days after the first injection, he was able to sit up in bed. The swelling in his face went down. Doctors felt Alexander was on the road to a full recovery. At this point, the doctors decided to stop treating Alexander with the drug.

For the next ten days, Alexander's condition continued to improve. Then things got worse. The infection returned. About a month after he had received the first injection, Alexander died.

Alexander might have lived if the doctors had been able to give him more of the drug. However, they had none left. What little they did have was being given to a fifteen-year-old boy who became the second patient to receive the drug. The boy had developed a serious infection following an operation on his hip. This time the drug was successful. The boy became the first patient to be saved by this new drug.

The doctors were thrilled by what had happened. Although they had used it on only two patients, the drug seemed perfectly safe to give to humans. More important, they had discovered that the drug could save lives. The doctors immediately began giving the drug to more patients with serious infections. The third patient was a man who had a very large infected area on his back. The man was very ill with a high fever and swollen glands. Seven days after first receiving the drug, the infection had completely disappeared.

The fourth patient to receive the drug was a four-year-old boy. One of his eyes had become infected after an attack of measles. The infection spread to the base of the boy's skull, causing his face to swell up. Nine days after first receiving the drug, the boy was talking and playing with his toys. Unfortunately, the boy died several days later from a weakened blood vessel in his brain. The doctors, however, saw that the drug had worked in curing the infection.

The fifth patient was a fourteen-year-old boy with a serious bone and kidney infection. Over a period of two weeks, the boy received the largest dose of the drug yet given. The result was a complete cure. The doctors started calling the new drug a "miracle."[2]

The "miracle drug" first used on these five patients was penicillin. The year was 1941. At that time, infections were a serious matter. Like Alexander, who got scratched by a rose thorn, people could die from a small cut that became

A newspaper headline proclaims the arrival of the new "wonder drug" penicillin in 1943.

infected. Doctors back then did have drugs to treat infections. These drugs, however, were not very effective, especially if the infection had spread. Penicillin changed everything.

Penicillin became the first drug that proved very effective in treating serious infections. Not only did it cure infections from scratches and cuts, penicillin also saved the lives of people suffering from certain diseases. One such disease is strep throat. Strep throat is caused by tiny living things called bacteria. Bacteria are so small that they can be seen only with the help of a microscope.

Despite their small size, many bacteria can cause huge problems, including serious diseases in humans. Some of these diseases can be deadly if they are not treated with a drug that can kill bacteria. Penicillin became the first drug that could quickly kill bacteria. Penicillin was the first to join a class of drugs called antibiotics. Today, doctors can choose from a large number of different antibiotics to treat infections and other diseases. In 1941, however, penicillin was their only choice. To make matters worse, penicillin was in very short supply. Remember that doctors did not have enough to treat Alexander because they gave all they had on hand to the fifteen-year-old boy.

Once doctors realized the value of penicillin, efforts began to make the drug in large amounts. A way also had to be found to make a purer drug. The first patients treated with penicillin had been injected with a liquid made with a

A man arranges bottles of incubated penicillin on shelves.

brown powder. This powder contained not only penicillin but several impurities that gave it a brown color.

At first, penicillin was made right in the hospital in a most unusual way. Penicillin came from a mold, like the mold that grows on stale bread. The mold was grown in a liquid kept in hospital bedpans. Pieces of silk fabric were cut from parachutes. The silk pieces were stretched across bookshelves. The liquid was drained from the bedpans and then filtered through the silk to get the penicillin. Obviously, the doctors needed a better way to make the large amounts of penicillin they needed. Drug companies were a logical choice.

The companies in England, however, could not help. All their efforts were already going to help England fight Germany in World War II. The doctors decided to fly to the United States for help. Their efforts were successful. The U.S. government led the drive to find new and better ways of growing the mold.

These new ways came just in time. On November 20, 1942, a fire broke out in the

The man who discovered penicillin: Alexander Fleming.

Coconut Grove nightclub in Boston. The fire killed 487 people. Many more people were injured. Large quantities of penicillin were quickly needed to treat over two hundred people who had been badly burned and needed skin grafts. The penicillin was used to prevent infections in the areas where the skin was grafted. This was the first large-scale use of penicillin.

The results were so successful that the U.S. government led the efforts to produce even larger quantities of penicillin. But the government kept the success of penicillin a secret for many years. It was worried that Germany might learn about penicillin and use it to treat their wounded soldiers. By the end of 1943, penicillin was being produced in huge amounts in the United States. Now there was enough penicillin to treat thousands of patients.

The first patients to be treated with all this penicillin were the Allied soldiers fighting in World War II. Doctors were saving these soldiers' lives by stopping the bleeding from their wounds. However, many of these soldiers later died from infections that started in their wounds. Once penicillin became available, all wounded soldiers were treated with the drug to prevent infections. The lives of countless soldiers were saved. In previous wars, many more soldiers had died from infections than from bullets. When treated with penicillin, 95 percent of the wounded in World War II lived.[3]

Penicillin was also used to treat soldiers who developed bacterial diseases. One such disease was pneumonia. During World War I, 18 percent of American soldiers who got pneumonia died from the disease. With the use of penicillin in World War II, less than one percent of American soldiers with pneumonia died from the disease.[4] By the end of World War II, the lives of millions of soldiers had been saved because of penicillin.

After the war ended in 1945, penicillin became available for civilians to use. Bacterial diseases that once caused fear were soon no longer a concern. If enough penicillin had been available in 1941, then Albert Alexander would not have any reason to worry about that scratch he got from a rose thorn. The story of penicillin, however, does not begin with Albert Alexander. Rather it begins with another Alexander: Alexander Fleming.

"Ah Cam Doun Tha Quick"

A STONE MONUMENT SITS HIGH ON A hill where very few people pass by. The writing on the monument reads, "Sir Alexander Fleming, discoverer of penicillin, was born here at Lochfield on 6th August 1881." Lochfield is a small farming village in the southwest region of Scotland. It was here that Alexander Fleming spent the first fourteen years of his life.

In 1855, Alexander's father, Hugh Fleming, came to Lochfield to farm. Hugh soon met and married Jane Young. Together Hugh and Jane managed the eight-hundred-acre farm where they raised sheep and cattle. They had four children: Jane, Hugh, Thomas, and Mary. Following the birth of their youngest child, tragedy struck the Fleming family. After delivering Mary, Jane became seriously ill and died. Now a widower, Hugh had to manage the farm and take care of four young children by himself.

Two years after his wife died, Hugh married Grace Morton. They had four more children: Grace, John, Alexander, and Robert. Alexander Fleming then was the second youngest of eight siblings. Raising all these children on a huge farm was no easy task. The only sources of heat were fireplaces that needed constant attention during the cold months. There was no running water, so bathing was saved for special occasions. The whole family shared only three bedrooms. On those nights when visitors stayed over, two or even three children had to share a single bed. No one, however, had to worry about sharing a bathroom. There was no bathroom in the house.

Jane, the oldest child from the first marriage, helped with many of the household chores. She liked taking care of her younger siblings, especially Alexander. Jane called him Alec, a nickname that would stick for life.

Jane was not the only one who had to help. All the children were given chores. The older the children were, the more responsibility they had. The younger children, including Alec, were given small chores that they could handle, like making sure the sheep did not wander too far.

Everyone was happy until tragedy again struck the Fleming family. When Alec was about two years old, his oldest sister Jane had married a doctor. Soon after her marriage, Jane came down with smallpox. At that time, smallpox was usually fatal. Despite all the loving care she received from her family, Jane died.

Still another tragedy struck when Alec was only five. His father suffered a stroke that left him paralyzed. All that Alec would remember of his father was an image of a gray-haired man who sat all day in a chair by the fire in the kitchen. A little more than a year after the stroke, Alec's father died.

Alec and his younger brother Robert grew very close after the deaths of their oldest sister and father. Both boys loved nature. Together they explored the hills and valleys of their farm. One game that they loved to play on their farm was rolling down hills. Alec and Robert often competed with each other to see who could roll down a hill the fastest. One day they picked a hill with a steep slope where the boys could roll really fast. However, rolling down this hill could mean disaster.

The hill ended suddenly with a sheer drop into a canyon filled with rocks and boulders. Falling into the canyon would mean certain death. Dared by his siblings, Alec decided to roll down the hill. As he tumbled down the hill, he was picking up more and more speed. Alec seemed to be out of control and headed for the canyon floor. Somehow he managed to twist his body just in time to stop at the bottom of the hill. A few more feet and he would have fallen to his death. When he got up, all Alec said in his thick Scottish accent was, "Ah cam doun tha quick."[1]

Alexander Fleming would always cherish what he learned about nature on his farm in the Scottish countryside.

Other adventures were much less dangerous for Alec and his younger brother. Their love of nature could be seen in how closely they watched and studied birds. They knew every kind of bird by name. In the spring they would collect eggs and sell them to a local grocer. The brothers made enough pocket change to buy such things as candy, but they were not greedy. They were always sure to leave enough eggs for the mother bird to hatch.

During the spring and summer, the boys also loved to fish. They used worms to attract the fish. The boys had to be very patient and remain absolutely still while they tried to bring the fish within reach. Once the fish was near enough, Alec or Robert would quickly reach down with one hand and grab it. Obviously, the boys were very fast with their hands.

Another sport they loved to play on their farm was hunting rabbits. They were too young to use guns. The brothers also felt that animal traps were cruel. So once again they had to depend upon their hands to catch their prey. Alec and Robert would go hunting for rabbits with their collies. Once the dogs had located a rabbit, the boys would walk past it pretending that they had not seen it. Then they would turn around suddenly, quickly dive on the rabbit, and grab it with their quick hands.

Although they sold the eggs they collected, Alec and Robert brought home the fish and rabbits they caught for dinner. Rabbits were used to make a stew with vegetables that were grown on the farm. Their hides were saved to make socks and mittens needed for warmth during the very cold winters in Scotland.

Winters were very harsh on the farm. Winds

could sometimes reach a hundred miles an hour. These strong winds would blow the snow into drifts twenty feet deep. Out in the fields, sheep would sometimes become completely buried by the snow. By huddling together with their wool coats, the sheep could survive for a few days. However, if the sheep could not get free by themselves, Alec's father and his older siblings would have to search for them. They looked for holes in the snow made by the warm breath of the sheep. Digging them out was always a challenge.

The Fleming family would also have to dig themselves out of their house whenever snowdrifts blocked the doors and windows. Even when they got out, they might not be able to go very far. The roads could remain closed for days because of the snowdrifts. The evenings in winter could be very long. However, the Fleming family had plenty to do. The children usually played games. They even invented some games to help pass the time. Alec, though, was approaching the age when playing games would be replaced by something more serious—school.

A Broken Nose

WHEN ALEC TURNED FIVE, HE STARTED attending a school that had just opened about a mile from the Flemings' farm. The school had only a single classroom with no more than fifteen students at any one time. The teacher, a woman in her early twenties, taught the children reading, writing, arithmetic, history, and geography.

In cold weather the children gathered around the fireplace in the classroom. Every day, each child had to bring one or two pieces of peat for the fire. Peat is a thick soil found in marshy areas, or bogs. When dried, peat burns well to provide a good amount of heat for warmth and cooking.

In warm weather the teacher and children gathered by the open window or down by the river. No matter what the weather was like, all the children walked to and from school every day. For Alec and his siblings, that meant walking about a mile in each direction. Whenever they had to walk through puddles or across muddy ground, the children would take off their shoes and socks. After arriving at school, they would dry their feet by the fire. Their shoes and socks would never have dried in time for them to walk back home.

Alec enjoyed learning in the one-room school where he spent five years. Later in life, he would say that he learned faster there than anywhere else. Proof of how well he had learned came when Alec turned ten. He was now old enough to move on to a larger school in the nearby town of Darvel. He did very well at this school and was often ahead of his classmates. One day, however, Alec found himself literally head-to-head with one of his classmates. The experience would remain with him for the rest of his life.

Playing in the school yard, Alec was running very fast around a corner of the building to get to his class. Running just as fast in the opposite direction was a classmate. The two collided head-on. The other boy's head hit Alec right in the nose, which quickly swelled up. When the swelling went down, Alec discovered that his nose had been badly broken. The accident left him with a flattened nose that he would have for the rest of his life.

The school in Darvel was about four miles from the Flemings' farm. Again Alec had to walk to and from school every day in all kinds of weather. In winter he had to walk both ways in darkness. The long walk also meant that he usually arrived cold and wet whenever it snowed or rained. Before he left home in such weather, his mother would give him two baked potatoes fresh from the oven. He kept one in each pocket to keep his hands warm. At school the baked potatoes would be part of his lunch.

A childhood accident left Fleming with a broken nose. Because of his flattened nose, people sometimes assumed that Fleming had once been a boxer.

Later in life, Alec thought that these long walks to and from school in all kinds of weather had a positive impact on his development. Amazingly, he rarely got sick as a child despite getting cold and wet so often. He felt that his good health and physical condition as an adult were the result of his tough upbringing as a child. These long walks also gave Alec the opportunity to observe nature as it changed from one season to the next. As an adult, he realized that he had "unconsciously learned a great deal from nature."[1] His ability to notice that something was different or unusual would prove very important later in life.

When he was twelve years old, Alec transferred to another school in Kilmarnock, a town far from the Flemings' farm. During the week, Alec stayed with an aunt who lived in the town. On weekends he went home by taking a train to a village about two miles from Darvel. He was usually able to get a ride from the village to Darvel, and then walk the four miles home. When he couldn't get a ride to Darvel, he had to walk from the train to his home, a distance of six miles. Alec would arrive home very late Friday night and start his journey back to school very early Monday morning.

Life for Alec in Kilmarnock was most interesting. Living in a town with about thirty thousand people was very different from living on an isolated farm where the nearest neighbors

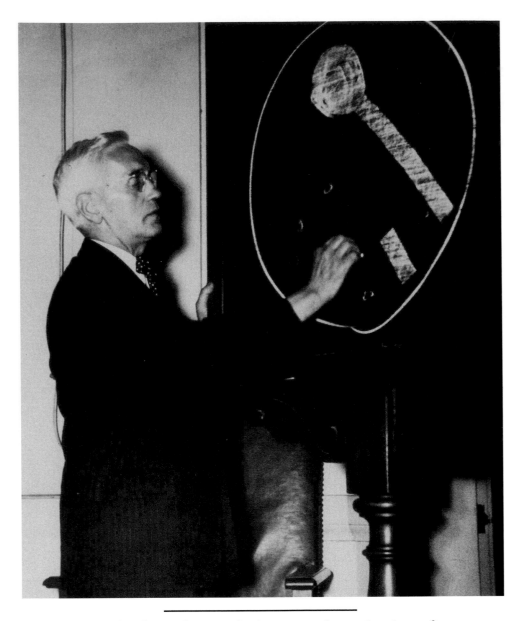

Alexander Fleming began to develop a strong interest in science after he transferred to a school in Kilmarnock, a town that was far away from the Fleming family farm.

were a mile away. The new school was also interesting and offered a variety of courses in foreign languages, mathematics, and science. In fact, science was emphasized at the school where students had to take two science courses each year. Alec developed a keen interest in science during his years in Kilmarnock.

Alec stayed at the school for only eighteen months. In the summer of 1895, Alec, now fourteen, was asked by his older brother Tom to live with him in London. Tom had gone to London where he had set up his practice as an eye doctor. His sister Mary had also moved to London with Tom to keep house for him. John, another brother, joined them a short while later. Six months after arriving in London, Alec was very happy when his younger brother Robert also came to live with them. Five Fleming siblings—Mary, Tom, John, Robert, and Alec—were once again living together as a family.

Alec and his siblings found London both fascinating and overwhelming. The city's underground subway had just been built. The house where the Flemings lived was located above the subway line. Every time a train passed underneath, the house would shake. Smoke from the steam engine would pour into the street, and some of it would find its way into their house.

During the day, the street where the Flemings lived was filled with horses. Horse-drawn carriages transported people. These carriages were the main means of getting around the streets of London before the automobile was invented. Horses also pulled wagons filled with meats and vegetables for sale by street vendors. At the end of the day, the smoke that drifted into the Flemings' house was replaced by the smell of horse manure.

Just as they had explored the land on their eight-hundred-acre farm, Alec and Robert decided to investigate London. Now they had the chance to visit museums, churches, parks, and the zoo. However, school still came first. Both Alec and Robert enrolled at the Polytechnic Institute. Their older brother Tom had decided that both boys should concentrate on studies that would prepare them for the business world. Despite his love of science, Alec bowed to his older brother's wishes.

During their first two weeks at the institute, Alec and Robert were judged to be two years ahead of their peers in their level of education. The school moved Alec up four classes. He became the youngest student in his class. Being the youngest was hard enough. As a Scot, Alec was also the target of jokes and pranks directed against him by his English classmates. Normally shy, Alec became even more withdrawn. Soon, however, his intelligence and charming Scottish accent earned him the respect of his class-mates.

Once again Alec received high marks in all his courses. In just two years, he easily passed all his courses. At the age of sixteen, he was finished with school and decided to look for work. He took a job in a shipping office in London. As a junior clerk, Alec copied letters and documents, entered numbers into accounting books, and prepared cargo lists.

Alec still lived with his family, who by this time had moved to another house in London. Their older brother Tom made sure that Alec and Robert continued their studies when they arrived home after work. He had the brothers each put up a coin and then asked them questions on history, geography, and math. The one who correctly answered the most questions got the money. Alec also enjoyed spending the evening with his family by playing Ping-Pong and cards. Work, however, was another matter.

Alec found his job as a shipping clerk very boring. He made few friends at the office where he worked for four years. Then, in early 1900, war broke out in South Africa, which was then an English colony. The war was being fought between the English and the Dutch (Boer) settlers living in South Africa. Alec decided to quit his job and enlist in the London Scottish Rifle Volunteers. His brothers Robert and John also enlisted.

None of the Fleming brothers were sent to South Africa to fight in the war. In fact, they

After moving to London in 1895, Alexander Fleming enrolled at the Polytechnic Institute, where he was judged to be two years ahead of his peers. He finished school by the time he was sixteen years old.

rarely left London. However, they were actively involved in their military units. Alec and Robert became expert marksmen and won shooting competitions. Although none of the brothers could swim when they came to London, Alec and Robert joined a military swimming club. Within a few months, both were such good swimmers that they made the water polo team. One polo match they played was against a team from St. Mary's Hospital. Little did Alec know at the time how important St. Mary's hospital would be in his future.

When the war ended, Alec went back to his job as a shipping clerk. Stuck in a job that he hated, Alec must have felt that his future was not very promising. Then, shortly before his twentieth birthday, something totally unexpected happened. Alec inherited some money from an uncle. In 1901 it was enough money for Alec to follow his brother Tom's advice to quit his job and go to medical school.

Two Obstacles

FLEMING WAS ALMOST TWENTY WHEN he decided to follow his brother's advice. He agreed, not because he always wanted to be a doctor, but only because he saw no future as a shipping clerk. However, there were two obstacles that Fleming had to overcome before being accepted by a medical school.

First, he was about three years older than students entering their first year of medical school. This age difference was not that big a problem, but the second obstacle seemed impossible to overcome. Fleming had never taken the entrance exam that every student had to pass before being accepted by a medical school. He also had never taken Latin, a course that was required by all medical schools. Determined to make a better future for himself, Fleming decided to hire a tutor to teach him Latin. He also enrolled in a school to take all the courses that he needed to prepare for the entrance exam.

In July 1901, Fleming took the exam. Not only did he pass everything, but he was also one of two students to receive the highest grades. Fleming was now eligible to attend any of the twelve medical schools in London. He chose St. Mary's simply because he had played a water polo match against their team when he was in the military.[1] Three months after passing the exam, Fleming started his medical studies at St. Mary's Hospital Medical School. He would remain associated with St. Mary's for the rest of his life.

When Fleming started his career as a doctor, the medical world had just made some remarkable progress. One of the major advances was the introduction of anesthesia in the 1850s. Before then, patients undergoing surgery had to bear the pain as best they could. The patient was strapped to the operating table. The surgeon worked as quickly as possible. An appendix, for example, would be removed in about two minutes. With anesthesia, a patient could be put to sleep and not be in any pain. The surgeon could take more time and therefore be less likely to make a mistake. Surgeons could also perform more complicated operations.

Another advance was the recognition that germs can cause disease. Starting in the mid-1800s, scientists from various countries began gathering evidence that germs caused certain diseases. These scientists included Louis Pasteur from France, Joseph Lister from England, Robert Koch from Germany, and Ignaz Semmelweis from Austria. The combined work of these scientists led to the germ theory. A theory is a widely accepted explanation of some observations. In this case the theory was simply that certain diseases were caused by germs. While

Alexander Fleming shakes hands with Dr. William Earl Clark, President of the Medical Society of the District of Columbia. Fleming's career in medicine began when he enrolled at St. Mary's Medical School in 1901.

this theory seems obvious today, it was quite difficult for people to accept in the mid-1800s.

The germ theory also stated that certain diseases could be prevented by either avoiding germs or killing them. In England, Lister searched for chemicals that would kill germs. He found one that was sprayed as a fine mist into the air of an operating room. The chemical worked. Fewer patients developed infections following their surgery. However, the chemical smelled awful, making many surgeons unwilling to use it.

In Austria, Semmelweis was especially concerned about the number of women who died in hospitals following childbirth. He felt that germs were responsible. Semmelweis noticed that doctors who delivered babies in the hospitals were coming straight from treating patients with various diseases. Using their hands to deliver the babies spread germs from these patients to the mothers. Many of the mothers died from what was called childbed fever. This disease was so common that many women feared going to the hospital to have their babies. Instead, they decided to have them at home with the help of midwives, who were women trained to deliver babies.

Semmelweis recommended that doctors wash their hands before delivering a baby. Today, this seems an obvious thing to do. In the 1860s, however, most doctors considered it an insult to be told to wash their hands. Semmelweis was so ridiculed for his suggestion that he had to leave the hospital where he worked. When Fleming entered St. Mary's in 1901, doctors in England did not have to wash their hands before delivering a baby. In fact, many doctors, including some at St. Mary's, still did not believe in the germ theory.

Having left school at sixteen, Fleming had to switch his frame of mind from the routines of work to the challenges of school. Just as he had done before, Fleming had no trouble learning. He was a model student from the start. At the beginning of his first year, he took the exam for the hospital scholarship and won it. The scholarship provided Fleming with enough money to cover his tuition.

At the end of his first year, he also won the prizes in biology and chemistry. In his second year, Fleming won two more prizes. His third year, he was appointed to the position of student prosecutor. This required Fleming to prepare a dead body for dissection and to use a pointer to show the other students the various parts as the professor spoke. His fourth year, he won three more prizes, including the Senior Anatomy Prize.

What is impressive is that Fleming earned high grades in medical school without studying all that hard. Still living with his family in London, he always had time in the evening to join in family games. A fellow medical student described how Alec managed to find the time to spend with his family. "He never burdened himself with unnecessary work, but would pick out from his textbooks just what he needed, and neglect the rest."[2] Fleming also had an excellent memory and found learning both interesting and fun.

Toward the end of 1904, with most of his exams behind him, Fleming continued his medical education in the hospital wards. In those days most of the patients were children and young adults with various types of infections. Even the doctors who believed in the germ theory had no good way to treat these infections. Antibiotics, such as penicillin, were not available. Fleming saw many patients suffering from strep throat, meningitis, tuberculosis, and pneumonia. Pneumonia often led to an even more serious infection of the chest. The only treatment available at that time was to remove several inches of one or more ribs. A tube was then inserted into the chest to drain the infection. This painful treatment could go on for weeks.

Another common and dangerous infection was just beginning to be recognized by doctors in the early 1900s. This was appendicitis. The only treatment is to remove the infected appendix. At that time, operating to remove an appendix was still risky. Thus, people with appendicitis were often unwilling to undergo the operation. One such person was Edward VII who was to be crowned king of England on June 26, 1901.

That morning he became suddenly ill with a high fever and pain in his abdomen. Both are signs of appendicitis. Doctors told the king that only an operation could save his life. He refused, saying that he must go to his coronation. When told that his condition was life threatening, he agreed to the operation. The badly infected appendix was removed, and the king was crowned a few weeks later. Surgery had saved the king.

Surgery was the field of medicine that Fleming wanted to pursue. In 1905, Fleming passed the exam to enter the Royal College of Surgeons. Here Fleming learned how to deliver babies. He also collected more prizes. In 1906, Fleming passed his final exams. He was now a doctor and qualified to open his own practice. However, there were some people at St. Mary's who did not want to see Fleming leave to set up his own practice. One such person was John Freeman.

Fleming sits between Major General S. U. Marietta (left) and Colonel Ash (right) of the Army Medical Museum during a trip to Washington, D.C., where Fleming was being honored for his discovery of penicillin. The road to this discovery began when Fleming joined the Inoculation Department at St. Mary's Hospital.

Like Fleming, Freeman was a member of the St. Mary's rifle club. Without Fleming, the club's chances of winning an upcoming major tournament were slim. So Freeman tried to convince Fleming to stay. One of the staff members at St. Mary's that Freeman highly respected was Almroth Wright. Wright was one of the doctors at the hospital who believed in the germ theory. Freeman knew that Wright had an opening in his department at the hospital. Freeman suggested to Wright that Fleming was the perfect person for the job.

In 1906, Wright asked Fleming to join his department. Freeman convinced Fleming to accept by telling him that "Wright's laboratory would make a good observation-post from which he could keep an eye open for a chance to get into surgery."[3] In any case, Fleming looked at the position as a temporary one. He was still determined to open his own practice as a surgeon. Fleming, however, would remain at St. Mary's for the next forty-nine years and never practice surgery.

Playing with Microbes

WRIGHT WAS IN CHARGE OF THE Inoculation Department at St. Mary's Hospital. Fleming became one of about eighteen staff members in his department. Half of this staff consisted of recent medical school graduates, like Fleming. The other half was made up of doctors from various parts of the world. No matter how young or experienced, everyone worked very hard.

Work began promptly at 9:00 A.M. Lunch was often eaten in the lab. An afternoon break was taken only so that Wright could discuss various matters with his assembled staff. Then it was back to work until dinner. After dinner everyone returned to the lab to work until midnight, when a short break was taken. This was an opportunity for the staff to discuss the day's work and plan for the next day. Sometimes it was two or three o'clock in the morning when the last person left the lab. The next day everyone would start all over again promptly at 9:00 A.M.

The work that kept everyone so busy in Wright's lab was their research on vaccinations. A vaccination is an injection given to protect a person against a particular disease. The first vaccination was developed in 1796 by an English doctor named Edward Jenner. At that time, many people died from a disease called smallpox. Those who survived were left with deep scars on their face. Jenner noticed that dairymaids, the women who milked cows, rarely got smallpox. Instead, they got a related disease called cowpox. Cowpox was not nearly as serious as smallpox, and it rarely left scars.

Jenner reasoned that cowpox somehow protected dairymaids against smallpox. To test his idea, Jenner inoculated, or injected, a young boy with the microbes, or germs, that cause cowpox. The boy developed cowpox. Months later, Jenner then injected the boy with the germs that cause smallpox. The boy never developed smallpox. The vaccination had worked. Unfortunately, most doctors and scientists ignored Jenner's work. Remember that the germ theory was not even accepted by everyone at the time Fleming was working in Wright's lab—more than one hundred years after Jenner's work.

A strong supporter of the germ theory, Wright had discovered a vaccine that protected against typhoid fever. This was a deadly disease that was spread by microbes present in contaminated food, milk, and water. Wright drove his staff to find vaccinations for more and more diseases. They tested their vaccines by injecting them into animals, and, at times, even into themselves. Fleming found himself slowly switching his interest from surgery to microbes.

His family couldn't help but notice this newfound interest. Whenever someone at home was sick with a sore throat or cold, Fleming would take throat and blood samples to examine in his lab at the hospital. He would then prepare a vaccine to inject into the sick member of his family. His brother Robert later wrote: "I must have had my arm punctured and injected with hundreds of different kinds of dead microbes in those days. Alec must have jabbed [dead] microbes into himself many more times. Here again Alec was a master of technique. He could insert the needle of a syringe into you so that you hardly felt it."[1]

Despite the hard work, Fleming never lost his love for games. He and his brother Robert played golf regularly. He once set up an indoor miniature golf course using every room in a friend's house. Fleming still belonged to the shooting team that won several competitions. Other activities that he enjoyed were painting and playing billiards.

Fleming's playful attitude could also be seen in the lab. He especially liked to draw pictures and designs using special bacteria that he had collected. Scientists grow bacteria on flat circular plates called petri dishes. The petri dishes are first filled with a hot gelatin-like substance called agar. The agar contains nutrients that bacteria need to grow. Like gelatin, agar hardens as it cools. Bacteria can then be smeared across the top of the agar. The plate is covered and placed in an incubator where the temperature is kept warm. Within a few days, the bacteria multiply so many times that they can be seen on the agar.

Fleming would smear the bacteria on the agar into the shape of a picture or design. After a few days in an incubator, the bacteria could be seen. The bacteria that Fleming used grew in various bright colors and formed miniature patterns on the agar. His love and enjoyment of his work would remain with Fleming for the rest of his life. Whenever he was asked what he did for a living, Fleming would say he "played with microbes."[2]

At times, this attitude irritated Wright, who felt Fleming treated his research too much like a game. Wright recognized, however, that Fleming

Alexander Fleming examines a petri dish. Petri dishes are used to grow bacteria.

was an intelligent, skilled, and dedicated doctor. For this reason, Wright gave Fleming an important assignment. In 1909, just three years after joining Wright's department, Fleming was asked to turn his attention to syphilis.

Syphilis is a disease that can be transmitted from one person to another through sexual contact. A mother can also pass the disease to her unborn child. In the early 1900s, doctors had no way to treat syphilis, which often led to death. At that time doctors were not sure what caused syphilis, although they suspected that microbes were responsible. Wright believed that if these microbes could be identified, then a vaccine to prevent syphilis could be developed. So he asked Fleming to work on this idea.

At the same time, a German scientist named Paul Ehrlich was working on a treatment for syphilis. His approach was different from Wright's idea of developing a vaccine. Ehrlich felt that a vaccine would be of no use to those who already had the disease. Rather, these people needed something to kill the microbes that caused syphilis. So Ehrlich searched for such a drug. He realized that he needed a drug that would kill the microbes but not harm the patient in any way. Ehrlich was looking for what doctors called a "magic bullet."[3]

Ehrlich tried hundreds of drugs. He tested these on mice and guinea pigs, which had been injected with the microbes that cause syphilis. Each test was numbered. At first, all the tests failed. The drug may have killed the microbes, but it also killed the animals. Finally test number 606 succeeded. The drug killed the microbes without harming the animals. Doctors throughout Europe hailed drug 606 as a "magic bullet." Ehrlich called it salvarsan.

Wright was one of the first people to receive samples of salvarsan from Ehrlich, who was a personal friend. Wright questioned the value of salvarsan, but he passed the samples on to Fleming, anyway. He instructed Fleming to test the drug on patients with syphilis.

Injecting the drug into patients was difficult. Salvarsan had to be injected into a vein rather than into a muscle. This way, salvarsan could quickly spread throughout the body and attack the microbes. Removing blood from a vein was something doctors had done for hundreds of years. However, injecting a drug into a vein was a procedure that had just been developed in the early 1900s. Very few doctors could do it. Fleming was one of them.

As a surgeon, Fleming had the skill needed to insert a needle into a vein quickly and without causing much pain. His use of salvarsan to treat syphilis proved very successful. Fleming quickly became known in London as the doctor who could treat syphilis. To deal with all the people seeking his services, Fleming set up a private practice. Up to this point, his salary from his job in Wright's department was enough to support himself. He was still living with family members in a house they shared in London. With his additional income, Fleming could now go out more often.

Fleming especially enjoyed going to the Chelsea Arts Club. Here he could enjoy good

Alexander Fleming stands in the middle of three officials of the U.S. government during a visit to Washington, where he was honored by the Medical Society of the District of Columbia. Fleming was one of the first doctors to regularly perform intravenous injections—injections through a vein.

food, lively conversations, and games. He was always ready to play any game, including cards, billiards, chess, and croquet. The club was limited to men. However, Fleming's social circle expanded to include women he met at dinner parties and social gatherings outside the club. He learned to dance. Although Fleming was shy and sometimes abrupt, many women found him warm and sensitive. His social and romantic life seemed to be getting underway when everything suddenly changed. Fleming was almost thirty-three years old when World War I broke out in 1914.

6

The War

ON JUNE 28, 1914, THE HEIR TO THE
Austrian throne was assassinated in Serbia. On
July 18, Austria declared war on Serbia. Russia,
Germany, and France soon joined the war. On
August 3, Germany invaded Belgium to attack
France. The next day, England, which had a
treaty with Belgium, entered the war. In less
than two months, a world war had started. World
War I would end with about 10 million soldiers
dead, some 20 million wounded, and another
million missing and presumed dead.[1]

Soon after England entered the war, Wright
offered to help. He volunteered the services of

his entire staff so that all British soldiers could be vaccinated against typhoid fever. Wright believed that this disease would quickly spread among the soldiers because of the unsanitary conditions in the trenches. At first, the British government saw no value in vaccinating its troops against typhoid fever. But Wright did not give up. After much effort, he finally convinced the government to vaccinate every British soldier. The lives of about 120,000 British soldiers are believed to have been saved because of Wright's efforts.[2]

Wright was also asked to study ways of treating wound infections. At the outbreak of World War I, surgeons were following the sanitary practices recommended by Joseph Lister. They sprayed the operating rooms with chemicals called antiseptics. These chemicals kill germs. The surgeons also cut wounds open, thoroughly cleaned them, and then wrapped them with bandages soaked with an antiseptic to kill any germs. This treatment could continue for days or even weeks. Only when there was no sign of infection did the surgeon suture the wound and allow the body to heal itself.

Despite all these precautions, many wounds still became infected. Efforts to treat the infections were mostly useless. Many infections lasted for weeks or even months. In most cases, the infection led to death. The problem was made worse by the explosives that were used for the first time in World War I. Bullets fired from machine guns, bombs dropped from airplanes, and shells shot from tanks all produced deep wounds. Small pieces of metal often buried their way into these wounds. Such wounds were likely targets for germs looking for a place to multiply.

Wright and his staff, including Fleming, were sent to France to see if they could find a better way to treat wound infections. They set up their lab in the basement of what was once a casino, a building used for gambling. Conditions for carrying out research were horrible. An overhead pipe leaked sewage. The rooms above, which were at one time filled with gamblers dressed in the finest clothes, now were filled with

Soldiers in World War I spent a good deal of their time in trenches where there was some protection from enemy fire, but little protection from unsanitary conditions and disease.

wounded soldiers in muddy and blood-soaked uniforms. Almost all the soldiers' wounds were dirty and infected.

Wright decided that their first job was to identify the bacteria that were responsible for most of the infections. He placed Fleming in charge. Fleming took samples from the wounds before, during, and after surgery. He closely examined the bullets, shell fragments, pieces of clothing, and anything else the surgeons removed from the wounds. Fleming also took samples of undamaged clothing from the wounded soldiers. He tested all these samples for bacteria. His findings were quite surprising.

Fleming discovered that the soldiers' own clothing was a major source of infection. Over 90 percent of the samples he tested were contaminated with bacteria that cause an infection called gangrene. Fleming reasoned that these bacteria got on the clothing from the horse manure used to fertilize the farmland where the soldiers camped. The only thing these bacteria needed was a way to move from the clothing on the outside to a warm place inside the body. A wound provided the perfect opening. Once inside the body, these bacteria could grow wild and cause an infection.

However, Fleming was confused as to how these bacteria could be growing inside a wounded area. Normally these bacteria do not grow when they are exposed to oxygen. How then could they grow in wounds that were open to the air? Fleming discovered that another type of bacteria was also growing in the wounds, but closer to the surface of the skin. These bacteria need oxygen to survive. Near the surface, they quickly used up oxygen and multiplied. Because they used up all the oxygen, these bacteria made it possible for the other type of bacteria to survive deeper in the wound where oxygen never reached. In 1915, Fleming published the first complete study of wound infections.[3] He described the bacteria that were responsible, what they needed to live, and how they caused infection.

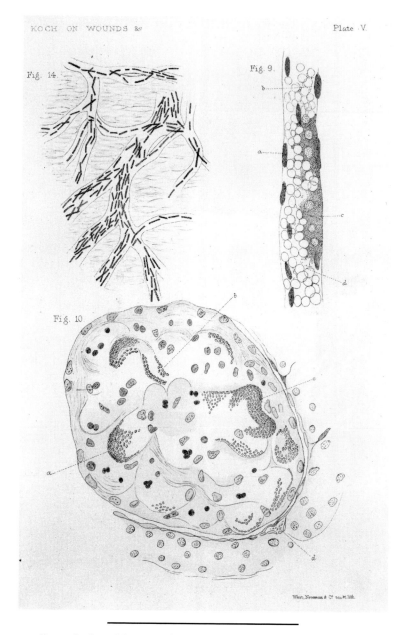

Bacteria found in wounds, as drawn from a photomicrograph.

In his study of wounds, Fleming made other valuable discoveries. He noticed, for example, that the area near a fresh wound was always filled with a type of white blood cell called a phagocyte. Fleming knew that phagocytes play an important role in fighting infection. They surround, swallow up, and destroy germs that enter the body. Fleming also looked for phagocytes in older wounds that had been treated with an antiseptic. He found that the area near these wounds had very few phagocytes. Fleming reasoned that the antiseptic was actually doing more harm than good. In fact, he showed that the antiseptic killed the phagocytes but left the bacteria unharmed.

His study of wounds also left Fleming puzzled as to how the antiseptic could quickly kill bacteria in a test tube but never in a wound. He reasoned that the antiseptic never got down into the wounds where the bacteria were growing. Surgeons found this hard to believe. Fleming somehow had to come up with a way to prove his idea. He thought of making an "artificial wound." With his talent for heating and bending glass, Fleming used a test tube to make such a wound. He heated the test tube and then pulled it to make a number of long and narrow spikes. Fleming had made a glass model of what a wound was really like.

He then poured a liquid filled with bacteria into the test tube. After a short time, he poured off the liquid. Next Fleming filled the test tube with an antiseptic solution. He left the antiseptic in the test tube for twenty-four hours. After pouring off the antiseptic, Fleming finally filled the test tube with a clear liquid. Within a short time, this liquid was filled with living bacteria. Fleming concluded the antiseptic solution never seeped into the narrow spikes to kill the bacteria living there. How then could an antiseptic applied on the skin kill bacteria deep inside a wound?

Supported by Wright, Fleming recommended a new procedure to treat wounds. First, he suggested that surgeons immediately stop the use of antiseptics. In their place, Fleming proposed that surgeons remove any dead tissue as quickly as possible, because it was a rich source of bacteria. He pointed out that "not only do dead tissues provide a good culture medium for microbes, [but] they actually prevent the healthy phagocytes from reaching them."[4]

Fleming recommended that the wound should then be treated with a germ-free salt solution to wash away bacteria and promote the growth of phagocytes. After closing the wound, the surgeon was to protect it with germ-free bandages. This new treatment worked well if done soon enough before an infection set in. But unfortunately it did little good on large or badly infected wounds. For this reason, most surgeons refused to follow Fleming's suggestions.

During World War I, Fleming published twelve papers on his study of wounds. Without a doubt, this made him the leading expert on wound infections. Yet, many of his suggestions were not followed by other surgeons during the war. However, Fleming's work became the basis for the standard treatment of wounds during World War II.

To take his mind off the tragedies of war, Fleming found games more important than ever. He played golf on Sundays. He and another doctor set up a putting course on the grounds of a hospital where they played at night by candlelight. Nothing, however, took his mind off his work more than Sarah McElroy. She was a nurse whom Fleming met while on leave in London. Her nickname was Sally.

At first, the two seemed an unlikely couple. Although the same age, Sally McElroy was bubbly and outgoing in contrast to Fleming, who was quiet and somewhat shy. While she loved to attend parties, he preferred to relax quietly with friends. Despite their personality differences, they were married on December 23, 1915. They were both thirty-four years old. The new couple rented an apartment in London, but Fleming soon had to return to his work at the hospital in France. His wife remained in London where she ran a nursing home that she had founded.

World War I officially ended on November 11, 1918. Although the war was finally over,

Fleming's work in the military was far from finished. In 1918 a serious disease broke out and soon spread throughout the world. The disease was Spanish influenza, named after the country where it was believed to have started. Fleming now switched his focus from war wounds to influenza, as the hospital filled up with soldiers suffering from this disease. Those who became infected had a mild fever one day and were often dead the next day. Their lungs would quickly fill with fluid, making breathing impossible. By the end of 1918, over 20 million people died from Spanish influenza.[5]

Although Fleming spent a year studying influenza, he never found either the cause or a cure. In January 1919, Fleming returned to St. Mary's Hospital in London. When he had left the hospital five years earlier, Fleming was known mainly for his work on syphilis. By the time he returned from the war, he had become the leading expert on infections. After what he had seen in France, he was now determined to find a way to cure them.

7

"A. F.'s Nose"

SOON AFTER HIS RETURN TO LONDON, Fleming was invited by the Royal College of Surgeons to give a talk about his work on infections. He presented what he had discovered, pointing out that antiseptics were useless in fighting infections. Unfortunately, Fleming's talk did not provoke much interest. The lack of response was likely due to Fleming's quiet and withdrawn manner. When speaking publicly, he never showed any emotion. His speech was always delivered in a rather flat, dull voice that was often difficult to hear. Fleming himself was very aware of his inability to keep his listeners interested in what he had to say. He often lamented not being a more magnetic speaker.

Shortly after returning to London, Alec and Sally Fleming moved. Their new apartment was near Fleming's brother John and John's wife, Elizabeth. Sally and Elizabeth were twin sisters who ran a private nursing home. Although married to John, Elizabeth was more like Alec. She and Alec were both reserved and usually quiet. In contrast, Sally and John were outgoing and talkative. The two couples spent many evenings together.

Two years later, Alec and Sally Fleming bought a house just outside the city. They spent the week in London living in their apartment while Fleming worked at the hospital. Every weekend, they drove out to their country house. Here Fleming was able to pursue his love for games and sports. He played tennis, croquet, golf, and billiards. He went fishing, swimming, and boating on a little river that wound through the property.

Fleming was not always comfortable giving public speeches. He often lamented not being a more magnetic speaker.

In 1921, Fleming was promoted to assistant director of the Inoculation Department at St. Mary's Hospital. His new job provided the Flemings with enough money to live comfortably. More important, this new job meant that Fleming could concentrate on his research and not worry about having a private practice. He never reopened the office he had set up in London to treat patients with syphilis. The lab at St. Mary's would be all that he needed.

Fleming shared the lab with another doctor named V. D. Allison. The two were quite different. Allison later wrote that "Fleming began to tease me about my excessive tidiness in the laboratory. At the end of each day's work I cleaned my bench, put it in order for the next day and discarded tubes and culture plates for which I had no further use. [Fleming], for his part, kept his cultures . . . for two or three weeks until his bench was overcrowded with forty or fifty cultures."[1] Allison goes on to say that if Fleming had been as neat as he was, then

Fleming would never had made his two famous discoveries. Penicillin was one. But first came lysozyme.

One evening in November 1921, Fleming showed Allison one of his cultures. As Allison recalled, "Discarding his cultures one evening, [Fleming] examined one for some time, showed it to me and said 'This is interesting.' The plate was one on which he had cultured mucus from his nose some two weeks earlier, when suffering from a cold. The plate was covered with golden-yellow colonies of bacteria. . . . The remarkable feature of this plate was that in the vicinity of the blob of nasal mucus there were no bacteria; further away . . . the bacteria had grown but had become . . . glassy and lifeless in appearance."[2] In other words, Fleming had noticed that the mucus from his nose had killed the bacteria on contact. The mucus could also affect bacteria growing some distance away on the petri dish.

Fleming had labeled the dish "A. F.'s nose," using his initials for the mucus samples. It seemed as if Fleming had discovered an antiseptic that was naturally present in his nose. He soon began to look for it elsewhere.

He tested mucus samples from the noses of other people. Fleming used bacteria that he got from the dish labeled "A. F.'s nose." All of them killed the bacteria. Next he tested tears. Fleming would squeeze lemon juice in his eyes in order to produce tears for his tests. He often recruited others to have lemon juice dropped in their eyes, as well.[3] Tears proved to be effective in killing the bacteria.

Fleming then checked saliva, blood, and even pus. Everything he tested killed the bacteria. During the next few weeks, Fleming experimented to see where else he could find this antiseptic. He tested every sample that he could get from patients in the operating room and from bodies in the morgue. The antiseptic seemed to be everywhere—in the skin, internal organs, nails, and even hair. Fleming also discovered it in rabbits, guinea pigs, horses, and dogs.

He also tested to see whether the antiseptic killed other types of bacteria, especially those known to cause disease. All the experiments where the antiseptic had worked were done with the bacteria that Allison had described as growing in "golden-yellow colonies." Fleming had named these bacteria "A. F. coccus." Coccus is a type of bacteria. Fleming had assumed that these bacteria were naturally present in his nose. Allison suspected that the wind had blown them in through a window in the lab and they had accidentally landed on the petri dish containing the mucus from Fleming's nose. Allison was probably correct.

In any case, these were harmless bacteria and posed no threat to human health. Fleming must have been extremely disappointed to discover that his antiseptic worked well only against harmless bacteria. Nonetheless he decided to present his findings in December 1921 at a meeting of the Medical Research Club. This group had been founded in 1881, the year Fleming was born. The members met on a regular basis to hear about recent discoveries in medicine, discuss their value, and suggest future experiments that might be worth doing.

As usual, the audience did not find Fleming's talk interesting. A question and answer period always followed a talk. But this time no one in the audience asked any questions when Fleming was finished speaking. He simply took his seat while the next speaker rose to address the audience. Although his listeners did not show any interest in what he had found, Fleming was still determined to pursue his work with this antiseptic.

He tested more samples from humans and various animals. He expanded his search to plants, including flowers and vegetables from the garden at his country home. Everything he tried contained the antiseptic. The vegetable with the highest concentration of the antiseptic was the turnip. Fleming later found an even better supply of the antiseptic. This was the white part of birds' eggs. He discovered that the white part of a bird's egg was a hundred times

Alexander Fleming (third from right) sits among a panel of officials during a visit to Washington, where he was honored by the Medical Society of the District of Columbia. Fleming was honored for his discovery of penicillin, but before that he had discovered lysozyme.

more powerful than tears in killing the bacteria. Fleming also found the antiseptic in the eggs of fish, including ones he caught in the river on his country property.

From his findings, Fleming concluded that every living thing must have this antiseptic. He decided to present his work not in a speech but in a scientific paper. This way, people might better appreciate his work by reading about it rather than by listening to one of his talks. Toward the end of January 1922, he sent his paper to Wright for approval. Wright immediately saw the value of Fleming's work. He agreed to submit Fleming's paper to the Royal Society, the world's oldest and most esteemed group of scientists.

But first Wright realized that the antiseptic needed a name. He called it lysozyme. *Lyso* came from the Greek word *lysis*, meaning "to dissolve," which is what the antiseptic did to the bacteria. *Zyme* came from the word enzyme. Enzymes are chemicals that cause certain changes to happen more quickly. Wright felt that the antiseptic worked like an enzyme, killing the bacteria very quickly.

Fleming's paper on lysozyme was published in 1922. Its title was "On a Remarkable Bacteriolytic Element Found in Tissues and Secretions." Everything suggested that

Fleming's work would finally be appreciated. Wright's talk at the Royal Society was enthusiastic. Fleming had called his discovery "remarkable." Yet, scientists at the meeting were again not impressed. They simply could not see the value of a chemical that only killed harmless bacteria.

To overcome this objection, Fleming searched for some practical benefit of lysozyme. He and Allison gave large doses of lysozyme by mouth to patients with intestinal infections. They found that lysozyme killed the bacteria in only one patient. Even then, this patient did not feel any relief from his symptoms. Fleming still did not give up.

In all, Fleming published eight papers on lysozyme, the last in 1932. He had spent eleven years investigating lysozyme. Despite all his work, Fleming could never show that lysozyme was an effective way to treat any infection caused by bacteria. Although lysozyme never did earn the label "remarkable," it continued to interest scientists long after Fleming had published his last paper. Today, lysozyme is added to various foods and wines to kill bacteria that otherwise might spoil them.

When Fleming discovered lysozyme in November 1921, he had a cold. He saw his cold as an opportunity to study the microbe that caused it. To do this, he took some of the mucus from his nose, placed it on a glass side, and examined it under a microscope. He also mixed the mucus from his nose with bacteria that probably blew in from an open window. Recall that Fleming's first clue that lysozyme killed bacteria came from petri dishes that he had not cleaned.

What if Fleming did not have a cold in November 1921? What if the window in the lab had been closed? What if Fleming always cleaned his petri dishes immediately after he examined them? Would he have discovered lysozyme? Probably not.

Fleming was not experimenting to see if the mucus from his nose killed bacteria. He discovered it purely by accident. The discovery of lysozyme is an example of serendipity. Serendipity is making an unexpected discovery by accident.

Fleming cannot be given credit for discovering lysozyme by planning a series of experiments with a purpose in mind. However, he can claim credit for his ability to notice what others might have overlooked. As a child walking to school, he always took the time to observe nature closely. In 1921 he used his keen sense of observation to discover lysozyme. In 1928 he would once again use his keen sense of observation to make another discovery. This time it would be penicillin.

Penicillin

IN SEPTEMBER 1928, FLEMING, HIS WIFE, Sally, and their four-year-old son, Robert, returned to London from their two-week summer vacation. Before leaving for vacation, Fleming had used some petri dishes to grow bacteria. As usual, he had simply put the dishes aside rather than clean them. Soon after his return, Fleming decided to straighten up his worktable. He cleaned the petri dishes by placing them in a disinfectant to kill the bacteria. Not wanting to miss anything, he always took a last look at his petri dishes before tossing them into the disinfectant. Not seeing anything of interest, he dumped them in the disinfectant.

That day, a former co-worker named D. M. Pryce stopped by to visit Fleming. Fortunately, some of the petri dishes had been stacked on top of others so that they were not covered by the disinfectant. Fleming picked up a few of these dishes to show Pryce what he had been doing. This time Fleming noticed something unusual. "That's funny," he said.[1] He pointed out an area on the dish to Pryce where no bacteria were growing. This clear area surrounded a large blob of yellow-green mold. Fleming realized that something from the mold had killed the bacteria. Unlike lysozyme that killed harmless bacteria, the mold killed bacteria that cause serious and sometimes deadly infections in humans.

Pryce, however, was not impressed. Fleming showed the petri dish to others in the lab, including Wright. They too were not impressed. Despite the lack of interest by his peers, Fleming remained excited about his discovery. But for some reason nearly two months passed before he conducted his next experiment with the mold. An entry in Fleming's lab notebook dated October 30, 1928, shows that he again found the mold effective in killing the bacteria.[2] This experiment was followed by others that filled up forty-eight pages in Fleming's lab notebook. To do all these experiments, he needed a steady supply of what he called "mold juice." He discovered that the mold belonged to a group of molds called *Penicillium*. For this reason, Fleming decided to call the active ingredient in the mold juice penicillin.

He soon discovered that penicillin killed different kinds of bacteria, including ones that cause pneumonia, meningitis, and diphtheria. Just as he had done with lysozyme, Fleming started looking for penicillin everywhere. He tested moldy cheese, jam, books, dirty clothes, and shoes. Only the mold that grew in his petri dish killed bacteria. Fleming, however, was not the first to discover that the *Penicillium* mold killed bacteria. This discovery was first made in 1875 and then again in 1925.[3] However,

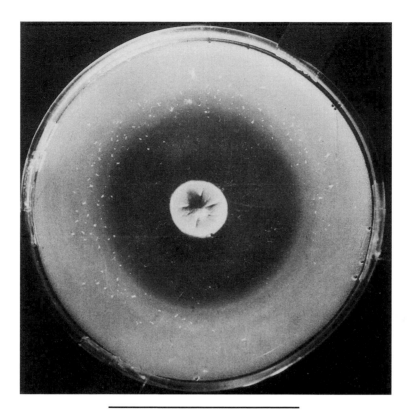

This Petri dish shows bacteria killed by penicillin amid live bacteria colonies.

Fleming was the first to recognize that the mold might be useful in treating infections.

On January 9, 1929, Fleming conducted his first experiment with penicillin on a human subject. A colleague named Stuart Craddock suffered from a serious sinus infection. He had undergone an operation where a tiny hole had been made so that his nose could always drain. However, Craddock's nose still became infected. At Fleming's suggestion, Craddock applied penicillin to the infected area twice a day for several days. There was no improvement.

The second human experiment was also a failure. Fleming applied penicillin to the open wound of a woman's leg that had been amputated in a car accident. The infection got worse, and the woman died. But then came success. In February an assistant in Fleming's lab had developed a serious eye infection. He was a member of St. Mary's rifle team and was set to compete in a shooting match. With the man's permission, Fleming applied the penicillin to the eye. The infection cleared up almost at once.

On February 13, 1929, Fleming gave a talk on penicillin at the Medical Research Club. He said, "I believe that penicillin although produced by a humble mold, will turn out to be a safe and most effective germ killer."[4] As usual, his talk made no impression. No one in the audience asked a question or made a comment. Several months

Penicillin was first discovered growing in this mold. The scientific name of this mold is Penicillium notatum.

later, Fleming published a report about his work with penicillin. His paper also drew little interest. By the summer of 1929, Fleming's interest was no longer focused on penicillin. But he did not entirely forget about penicillin.

Fleming continued to grow it in cultures. He sent samples to scientists working in other labs. At times, he still experimented with penicillin to see if it could be used to treat infections. Eventually, however, Fleming became convinced that penicillin would never become the "magic bullet" that would cure infections. In a talk he gave in 1945, Fleming said, "We tried it [penicillin] tentatively on a few old sinuses in the hospital, and although the results were favorable, there was nothing miraculous."[5]

Fleming's comments in 1945 are quite surprising in view of what had happened four years earlier. Remember that in 1941 doctors were using the term "miracle" because of what had happened to the five patients whose infections had responded to penicillin. The penicillin used to treat these patients was very different from the penicillin that Fleming had used in his tests with humans. The penicillin that had worked was purer and more powerful than Fleming's. This more powerful penicillin was the result of work done by two men working at

A photo of Howard Florey. Florey was born in Australia, studied in America, and moved to England in 1927.

Oxford University, about fifty miles from Fleming's lab at St. Mary's Hospital. One of these men was a doctor named Howard Florey. The other was a scientist named Ernst Chain.

Florey and Chain first became interested in penicillin after reading Fleming's paper that had been published in 1929. In 1938 they began to focus their work on penicillin. A year later, Florey applied to the Medical Research Council in London for the money they needed to carry out their experiments with penicillin. But three days earlier, Britain had declared war on Germany and had little money to spare for medical research. As a result, Florey got only a small amount of the money he requested. Realizing that it was not enough for all the experiments he had planned, Florey applied to the Rockefeller Foundation in New York City. Impressed by his proposal, the foundation gave Florey enough money to carry out his experiments for five years—two years more than he had requested.

Florey and Chain's first goal was to develop a way of getting a purer penicillin. By March 1940 they had enough penicillin to begin testing. Their penicillin was far purer than anything Fleming ever had. They checked to see if their penicillin was safe to use by injecting it into two healthy mice. The mice lived. This was nothing new. Eleven years earlier, Fleming had injected his penicillin into mice, and they too lived. But what Florey and Chain did next was something that Fleming had never tried. They injected penicillin into sick animals.

On the morning of May 25, 1940, Florey injected eight mice with bacteria that cause a deadly disease. Four of the mice were put back into their cages. The other four were given injections of penicillin. By the time of the last injection that night, the four untreated mice were all dead. The treated mice were all fine. The following day they repeated the same experiment, this time using ten mice. The five that were not treated died. The five that got penicillin lived. Their next experiment involved fifty mice. Of the twenty-five that got penicillin, twenty-four lived. Florey said, "It looks like a miracle."[6]

In August 1940, Florey and Chain published the results of their experiments. Fleming had no idea that anyone was experimenting with penicillin until he read their paper. Fleming immediately contacted Florey to see if he could visit them to discuss their work. Chain was shocked. As he put it, "Fleming? Good God, I thought he was dead."[7]

Almost twelve years to the day after he first discovered penicillin, Fleming visited with Florey and Chain. Upon meeting them, Fleming said, "I've come to see what you've been doing with my old penicillin."[8] Florey took Fleming on a tour of the lab, showing him how they purified the penicillin. Fleming had few questions or comments. He told Chain before leaving that he was glad that they made such good use of his work.

Florey and Chain pressed harder in their efforts to make an even purer and more powerful form of penicillin. They realized that a sick human would need three thousand times the dosage of penicillin used on a sick mouse. Finally, in February 1941, they were ready. Albert

A photo of Ernst Chain. Chain was born in Germany and fled to England when the Nazis came to power in 1933. In 1935, Chain and Howard Florey started working together at Oxford University.

Alexander, the London policeman who had scratched his face with a rose thorn, became the first patient to receive this purer and more powerful penicillin. The use of penicillin to treat infections and bacterial diseases would now become part of the medical world.

By May 1943 penicillin was used regularly during World War II to treat Allied soldiers who were either wounded or suffering from a bacterial disease. The results were amazing. For example, during World War I, some 70 percent of wounded limbs had to be cut off because of infection. During World War II, only 20 percent had to be amputated.[9] Fleming, with his experiences of World War I, was even impressed by penicillin's impact during World War II. Speaking of soldiers who quickly recovered from their wounds because of penicillin, Fleming said, "They didn't even have raised temperatures."[10]

While Florey and Chain were busy getting large quantities of pure penicillin for the war effort, Fleming had not forgotten his discovery. In August 1942, Fleming called Florey to ask if he could spare any penicillin. A worker at Robert Fleming's business had developed meningitis and was dying. Florey sent Fleming his entire supply of penicillin. At first, Fleming injected the penicillin into the man's muscles. His condition did not improve. Then Fleming tried something that had never been done before. He injected some penicillin directly into the man's spine where the disease was centered. Penicillin saved the man's life.

That same year, penicillin caught the public's attention. On August 27, 1942, a London newspaper carried a story about penicillin in a leading article. Soon other newspapers picked up the story. But none of the newspapers mentioned the names of either Fleming, Florey, or Chain. Then, on August 31, a letter from Wright appeared in one of the newspapers. Wright wrote that Fleming "is the discoverer of penicillin and was the author also of the original suggestion that this substance might prove to have important applications in medicine."[11] This letter brought Fleming to the world's attention.

A World Hero

SHORTLY AFTER WRIGHT'S LETTER appeared in the newspaper, Fleming became the focus of attention in England. Newspapers all over the country told of his amazing discovery. One paper named him "Man of the Week." In 1943, at the age of sixty-two, Fleming was elected as a Fellow of the Royal Society, the greatest honor that his peers could give him. The next year Fleming was made a member of the Royal College of Physicians. That same year he was knighted by the king of England. From that moment he had the right to be addressed as Sir Alexander Fleming.

On May 7, 1945, World War II in Europe ended. That same year, Fleming's status as a world hero began. In June he and Sally toured the United States. Everywhere he went he was mobbed by reporters. In Washington, D. C., Fleming was given a banquet in his honor by senators and cabinet members. In Boston he was asked to deliver the commencement speech at Harvard University where he was also awarded an honorary degree of doctor of science. In New York he was the guest of honor at a dinner held at the Waldorf Astoria hotel.

Fleming then traveled to Canada where he toured its penicillin plants. After returning to England for just a short time, he was next invited to France as a guest of the government. There he addressed the French Academy of Medicine in Paris and received the Legion of Honor, France's highest award. He also traveled to Italy where he met with the pope and to Belgium where he got three honorary degrees in two days. In all, Fleming received 26 medals, 25 honorary degrees, 18 prizes, 13 decorations,

Penicillin helped save the lives of many Allied soldiers in World War II.

and honorary memberships in 89 academies and societies.[1] Of all these awards, the greatest honor was given by Sweden—the 1945 Nobel Prize for Physiology or Medicine.

The Nobel Prize was actually awarded to three people that year. The other two were Florey and Chain. After the awards ceremony,

Fleming wrote: "Early to bed it should have been, but when we got back to our hotel we adjourned to the bar and drank Swedish beer for a long time."[2] He did not get to bed until 3:00 A.M. The next morning, Fleming, like all the other Nobel Prize winners, had to give a speech. In it, he said that "penicillin started as a chance observation. My only merit is that I did not neglect the observation."[3]

Fleming never hid the fact that he had discovered penicillin by serendipity. Like his discovery of lysozyme, he had not planned a series of experiments with the hope of finding an antiseptic that would kill dangerous bacteria. He found penicillin only because the petri dish with the *Penicillium* mold never made it into the disinfectant. He had even failed to observe it the first time he looked at the dish. What if Fleming had cleaned the petri dishes before leaving for his summer vacation? What if his former co-worker Pryce had not visited the lab after Fleming returned? Would Fleming have simply taken the petri dish and made sure it got soaked

Alexander Fleming receives the Nobel Prize from King Gustav of Sweden.

in the disinfectant? The answers to these questions will never be known. But we do know that Fleming was hailed as a world hero.

On the other hand, Florey and Chain went largely unrecognized. This was no fault of Fleming's. Shortly after Wright's letter appeared in the newspaper, another letter was published pointing out the work done by Florey and Chain. After reading this letter, Fleming wrote Florey to say: "I was very glad to see [the] letter in the [paper] this morning. Although my work started you off on the penicillin hunt, it was you who have made it a practical proposition, and it is good that you should get the credit." Fleming goes on to point out that he did not seek the publicity he was receiving. "You [Florey] are lucky in Oxford to be out of range of reporters. They are a persistent lot, and I have not been able to dodge them completely."[4]

For the most part, the media was responsible for Fleming receiving worldwide recognition. Shortly after Wright's letter appeared, hundreds of articles appeared in newspapers throughout the world. Nearly everyone mentioned Fleming's name. Only a very few carried the names of Florey and Chain. Florey himself was partly to blame. When the press did go to Oxford to speak to Florey, he refused to see them. He felt that any publicity would create a huge demand for penicillin, which was still very limited. "He [Florey] believed it would be immoral to raise hopes only to dash them."[5] As a result, the public in the 1940s read about penicillin as if Fleming had been solely responsible for discovering what it could do.

The Nobel Prize also carried a cash award that would be worth $130,000 today. This money was divided among Fleming, Florey, and Chain. This would be most of the money that Fleming ever made from his work with penicillin. Others, especially the drug companies that manufactured penicillin, would make millions. This made many people wonder. In fact, one of these people was the head of a drug company that was making huge profits from penicillin. He asked Fleming, "Why have you never touched the [moneys] which could have enabled you and yours to live as a man should live who has rendered such services to humanity?" Fleming simply answered, "It never occurred to me."[6]

Actually, Fleming was prohibited by English law from making any money from the sales of penicillin. The law prevented him from claiming any personal benefits because he did not invent penicillin. It is a natural substance produced by a mold. In addition, Fleming did not invent any new method for isolating or manufacturing penicillin. Whenever Fleming was offered money, he usually did not accept. For example, after he spoke in New York, the penicillin producers handed him a check for $100,000. This is equal to almost $1 million today. Fleming protested, saying that he could not possibly keep the money for himself. So he asked that the money be used for research by his department at St. Mary's Hospital.

At first, Fleming was upset by all the attention he received. He wrote to Florey: "For the moment, I am the sufferer."[7] Gradually,

Fleming realized that he had no choice. He had to learn to cope with reporters and make speeches.

Fleming learned quite well. He became very comfortable being around people, including reporters. Once while walking into his hotel in New York, two reporters surrounded him and asked, "What are you thinking of at this moment? We want to know what a great scholar thinks about before breakfast." Fleming replied, "I was wondering whether I would have one egg for breakfast, or two."[8] Up to this point in his life, he never liked getting up to speak before an audience. Now he could address an audience of six thousand people at Harvard University where everyone rose to greet him, cheering and clapping for several minutes.

Nearly twenty thousand people rose and cheered wildly when Fleming and his wife attended a soccer match in Spain in 1948. He had been invited to Spain to receive even more honors. But this trip would be marked by tragedy. Suddenly one evening in June, Sally

Fleming is seated near the head of the table at the Mayflower Hotel, where he was honored by the Medical Society of the District of Columbia. As time went on, Fleming became much more comfortable making speeches at such public events.

became ill. She had to spend most of her time in her hotel bed with a fever. After her return to England, she was no longer able to travel with Fleming to the ceremonies and dinners that continued in his honor. Sally was soon hospitalized, and then had to be placed in a nursing home when doctors could no longer do anything for her. Fleming told a friend, "The most horrible thing about it is that penicillin can do nothing for her."[9] Sally died on October 28, 1949. The exact cause of her death is not certain. They had been married for thirty-four years.

Fleming was overcome with grief. For the first time in his life, he kept the door to his office in his lab shut. His son, Robert, now twenty-five, was his only comfort. But Robert was often away from home completing his medical studies at St. Mary's Hospital. Then in 1951, Robert joined the army, leaving his father completely alone once again. The only way to keep his mind off his recent loss was to work in his lab. Returning to work in his lab would also mark the start of a new life for Fleming.

One of the most devoted workers in his lab was Amalia Voureka. She was a Greek widow who had started working in the lab in 1946. After Sally's death, Amalia and Fleming began working on research projects as a team. The two published scientific papers together. Amalia spoke several languages, and she soon began serving as Fleming's interpreter when non-English-speaking guests visited the lab. In April 1953, Fleming, now seventy-one, married Amalia. Like Sally, Amalia accompanied Fleming as he continued to travel around the world to receive more prizes and awards.

Then one day in October, Fleming woke up in the middle of the night with a high fever. He suspected that he had pneumonia. Tests at St. Mary's confirmed his suspicion. His doctor gave him an injection of penicillin. Within two hours he began to feel better. By twelve hours he was almost back to normal. The bout with pneumonia convinced Fleming to give up a life-long habit—smoking. He had once smoked as many as sixty cigarettes a day.

As soon as Fleming recovered from pneumonia, he was once again traveling around the world. On March 17, 1955, he was to begin a trip to Turkey and Greece. But by now ten years of countless dinners, ceremonies, and parties were beginning to take its toll. Fleming asked Amalia whether they should cancel their

This wartime poster boasts the virtues of penicillin as a "life-saving drug."

trip. On the morning of March 11, he came out of the bathroom looking so pale and sick that Amalia was alarmed. She told him to lie in bed while she called their family doctor. The doctor asked if he should cancel his other appointments and come by at once. Fleming did not feel that his condition was that serious. He answered, "No urgency whatever. See your other patients first."[10] As he and Amalia spoke quietly, his head suddenly fell forward. Alexander Fleming died of a heart attack on March 11, 1955, at the age of seventy-three.

Fleming once said, "I can only suppose that God wanted penicillin, so He created Alexander Fleming."[11]

Activities

In Fleming's Footsteps

In the 1940s penicillin was the only antibiotic available. Today, there are many antibiotics that a doctor can choose from to treat a bacterial infection or disease. Since the work of Fleming, Florey, and Chain, efforts to kill bacteria have extended beyond the medical world. Antiseptics are now added to an increasing number of household products. For example, some liquid soaps have an ingredient to kill bacteria. These soaps often include the word "antibacterial" on their labels. You can experiment to see how well these soaps kill bacteria.

A Recipe for Bacteria

Heat some chicken broth until it begins to boil. Keep the broth simmering for one minute. Then allow it to cool. While the broth is cooling, thoroughly clean two small glass jars with liquid soap and water. Be sure to rinse the jars thoroughly with running water. Label one jar "A," the other "B." Half fill both jars with chicken broth. Add one teaspoon of sugar to each jar. Stir the broth until the sugar dissolves. The chicken broth and sugar will provide the nutrients that bacteria need to grow and multiply.

Add one teaspoon of liquid soap to the jar labeled "A" and stir gently. Place both jars in a spot where they are exposed to the air. Bacteria in the air will fall into the open jars. If these bacteria start to grow and multiply, you will notice that the broth turns cloudy. If the liquid soap is effective, the broth should remain clear— at least longer than the broth that has no liquid soap. Experiment to determine how much soap is needed to slow down or prevent the growth of bacteria. You can either add more soap at the beginning or add a little each day as your experiment progresses. Keep a record in a notebook, just as Fleming kept a record in his notebook of exactly what he did.

If bacteria grow in the broth, be sure that you do not come in contact with the broth. Also be sure that none of the broth spills. The bacteria growing in the broth may be capable of causing disease. When you are finished with your broth, put on a pair of rubber or plastic kitchen gloves and fill each jar with liquid bleach. Allow the jars to remain undisturbed for twenty-four hours. The bleach will kill the bacteria. Once the bacteria have been killed, you can pour the contents down a drain and flush thoroughly with running water. Rinse the jars with running water before placing them in the garbage.

Antibacterial Agents

Liquid hand soap is not the only household product that contains an ingredient to kill bacteria. Other products include hand lotions, dishwashing detergents, sponges, kitchen cutting boards, plastic wrap for foods, pillows, sheets, mattress pads, socks, athletic shoes, toothpastes, and even toys. The active ingredient in most of these products is an antibacterial chemical called triclosan. Triclosan is even added to the metal used to make small kitchen appliances such as toasters and mixers.

Check your local supermarket. Look closely, just as Fleming did. Read the labels to see how many household products you can find that contain an antibacterial ingredient. Also check the Internet. Use a search engine and type in the keyword "triclosan" or the phrase "antibacterial ingredient household product." How many of these products do you have in your home? Locate information on why antibacterial ingredients are added to household products.

It would seem that bacteria do not stand a chance of surviving in a household equipped with all these products. In fact, using these products would seem to guarantee a germ-free household. However, scientists have expressed a serious concern about the increasing number of household products that contain an antibacterial ingredient. One concern is that these products destroy good bacteria as well as those that cause disease. Another concern is that these products cannot kill all the harmful bacteria. What happens next may be a serious threat to human health.

Those bacteria that are not killed are said to be resistant to the antibiotic or antiseptic. These resistant bacteria survive and continue to produce more bacteria. The bacteria they produce are also likely to be resistant. If the antibiotic is used over and over, then all that will survive are resistant bacteria. Obviously, at some point the antibiotic will do little, if any, good. This is exactly what has happened.

Dangers of Overuse

More than two thirds of bacterial infections in hospitals in the United States do not respond to at least one of the antibiotics that used to work. About half of bacterial infections in people treated but not admitted to hospitals also do not respond. For the first time, there are five types of bacteria that are resistant to every known antibiotic.[1] If anyone should develop an infection from one of these five bacteria, then treatment with an antibiotic would be useless. An infected person would have to depend totally on their own defense mechanisms to kill the bacteria. If these mechanisms should fail, then the person will be in the same situation as Albert Alexander. His infection from a minor scratch eventually killed him.

Doctors are becoming more and more concerned about the increasing number of bacteria that are becoming resistant to antibiotics. They are particularly disturbed about a type of bacteria that causes pneumonia, which can be life threatening to adults and especially children. Ten years ago, only 0.02 percent of these bacteria were resistant to penicillin. In 1996 that number jumped to 27 percent.[2] In addition to pneumonia, doctors are also concerned about antibiotic-resistant cases of ear infections, meningitis, blood infections, and food poisoning. From 1996 to 1998 there were thirteen cases of severe food poisoning that were resistant to the antibiotic used to treat this infection. These were the first antibiotic-resistant food-poisoning cases reported in the United States.[3]

When antibiotic-resistant bacteria are present, doctors must often look for other ways to treat an infected patient. Drugs may be given to help the body's defense mechanisms fight the infection or disease. The patient may have to be placed in a hospital to reduce the chances of exposure to other bacteria. Whatever happens, antibiotic-resistant bacteria have resulted in higher medical costs. It is estimated that antibiotic resistance costs the United States health care system between $100 million and $30 billion each year.[4]

To overcome the problem of antibiotic resistance, scientists are busy trying to find new drugs that can kill disease-causing bacteria. Their search will not be easy. In the meantime, many doctors are advising people to avoid taking any antibiotic unless it is absolutely necessary. It is estimated that half of all antibiotics prescribed by doctors are unnecessary.[5] In some cases, the antibiotic prescribed cannot fight the disease. In other cases, the patient may have a disease caused by a virus, against which antibiotics are useless. For example, a review of 28,000 patients with colds or upper-respiratory infections showed that half of them were given an antibiotic. In every case, the antibiotic was useless. Colds and upper-respiratory infections are caused by viruses. There are only a few other ways to kill viruses other than depending on the body's own defense mechanisms.

Hollie's Story

Hollie Mullin, a three-week-old baby, was sick. Her parents thought she had an ear infection. The doctors, however, were not sure she did. But Hollie's parents insisted that the doctors do something. So they gave Hollie repeated dosages of antibiotics to treat an ear infection. These repeated dosages probably allowed at least one antibiotic-resistant strain to develop in her ears. When Hollie did develop a definite ear infection, all the antibiotics given by mouth did not work. Doctors had to put Hollie in the hospital for two weeks where an antibiotic was slowly dripped into one of her veins.[6]

Like some of the first patients treated with penicillin, Hollie recovered from her infection. But unlike those first patients in the 1940s, Hollie, like everyone else today, must be careful before taking an antibiotic. Imagine what Fleming might have said if he knew that overuse of his miracle drug would one day lead to a health concern for humans.

Chronology

1881—August 6: Alexander is born to Hugh and Grace Fleming in Lochfield, Scotland.

1886—Alec begins his education in a one-room schoolhouse.

1888—Hugh Fleming dies from a stroke.

1895—Alec and his brother Robert attend the Polytechnic Institute where they take business courses.

1897—Alec takes a job as a shipping clerk in London.

1900–1901—Fleming and his brothers Robert and John enlist in the London Scottish Rifle Volunteers to fight in the Boer War.

1901—Fleming attends St. Mary's Hospital Medical School.

1906—Fleming graduates from medical school and joins Almroth Wright's department at St. Mary's.

1914–1919—Fleming becomes an expert on wound infection while serving in France during World War I.

1915—December 23—Fleming marries Sarah "Sally" McElroy.

1921—Fleming discovers lysozyme.

1924—The Fleming's only child, Robert, is born.

1928—Fleming discovers penicillin.

1929—Fleming gives penicillin for the first time to a human subject.

1941—Albert Alexander is the first person to be injected with a purer and more powerful form of penicillin developed by Howard Florey and Ernst Chain.

1942—Letter from Almroth Wright appears in a London newspaper giving credit to Fleming for having discovered penicillin.

1945—Fleming receives international recognition, including the Nobel Prize in Physiology or Medicine that he shares with Florey and Chain.

1949—Sally Fleming dies.

1953—Fleming marries Amalia Voureka.

1955—March 11—Fleming dies from a heart attack at the age of seventy-three.

Chapter Notes

Chapter 1. The First Patients

1. Dr. Simon Torok, "Howard Florey—Maker of the Miracle Mould," n.d., <http://www.abc.net.au/science/slab/florey/story.htm> (April 12, 2001).

2. Gwyn Macfarlane, *Alexander Fleming: The Man and the Myth* (Cambridge, Mass.: Harvard University Press, 1984), p. 186.

3. David Ho, "Alexander Fleming," *Time*, March 29, 1999, pp. 117–119.

4. "Penicillin, the Wonder Drug," n.d., <http://www.botany.hawaii.edu/faculty/wong/BOT135/Lect21b.htm> (April 12, 2001).

Chapter 2. "Ah Cam Doun Tha Quick"

1. Gwyn Macfarlane, *Alexander Fleming: The Man and the Myth* (Cambridge, Mass.: Harvard University Press, 1984), p. 12.

Chapter 3. A Broken Nose

1. *A Science Odyssey: People and Discoveries: Alexander Fleming*, n.d., <http://www.pbs.org/wgbh/aso/databank/entries/bmflem.html> (May 16, 2001).

Chapter 4. Two Obstacles

1. Gwyn Macfarlane, *Alexander Fleming: The Man and the Myth*. (Cambridge, Mass.: Harvard University Press, 1984), p. 26.

2. André Maurois, *The Life of Sir Alexander Fleming*, trans. Gerard Hopkins (New York: E. P. Dutton, 1959), p. 31.

3. Ibid., p. 37.

Chapter 5. Playing with Microbes

1. Gwyn Macfarlane, *Alexander Fleming: The Man and the Myth* (Cambridge, Mass.: Harvard University Press, 1984), p. 69.

2. "Alexander Fleming (1881–1955)," *WWW Style Sheet*, n.d., <http://clio.cshl.org/public/History/scientists/fleming.html> (May 16, 2001).

3. "Paul Ehrlich: Florey and Chain, the Development of Penicillin," n.d., <http://www.schoolshistory.org.uk/paulehrlich.htm> (May 16, 2001).

Chapter 6. The War

1. William L. Langer, *An Encyclopedia of World History*, 5th edition (Boston: Houghton Mifflin, 1972), p. 976.

2. Gwyn Macfarlane, *Alexander Fleming: The Man and the Myth* (Cambridge, Mass.: Harvard University Press, 1984), p. 82.

3. Ibid., p. 86.

4. André Maurois, *The Life of Sir Alexander Fleming*, trans. Gerard Hopkins (New York: E. P. Dutton, 1959), p. 86.

5. Macfarlane, p. 93.

Chapter 7. "A. F.'s Nose"

1. Gwyn Macfarlane, *Alexander Fleming: The Man and the Myth* (Cambridge, Mass.: Harvard University Press, 1984), p. 99.

2. Ibid.

3. Ed Hird, "Countless Millions Saved," n.d., <http://www3.telus.net/st_simons/cr0002.htm> (May 16, 2001).

Chapter 8. Penicillin

1. W. A. C. Bullock, *The Man Who Discovered Penicillin* (London: Faber and Faber, 1963), p. 73.

2. Gwyn Macfarlane, *Alexander Fleming: The Man and the Myth* (Cambridge, Mass.: Harvard University Press, 1984), p. 120.

3. David Ho, "Alexander Fleming," *Time*, March 29, 1999, p. 117.

4. André Maurois, *The Life of Sir Alexander Fleming*, trans. Gerard Hopkins (New York: E. P. Dutton, 1959), p. 136.

5. Macfarlane, p. 139.

6. Bullock, p. 91.

7. "Medicine's Accidental Hero," *U. S. News & World Report,* August 24, 1998, p. 62.

8. Ibid.

9. Bullock, p. 98.

10. Macfarlane, p. 209.

11. Ibid., p. 198.

Chapter 9. A World Hero

1. Ed Hird, "Countless Millions Saved," n.d., <http://www3.telus.net/st_simons/cr0002.htm> (May 16, 2001).

2. André Maurois, *The Life of Sir Alexander Fleming*, trans. Gerard Hopkins (New York: E. P. Dutton, 1959), p. 212.

3. W. A. C. Bullock, *The Man Who Discovered Penicillin* (London: Faber and Faber, 1963), p. 105.

4. Gwyn Macfarlane, *Alexander Fleming: The Man and the Myth* (Cambridge, Mass.: Harvard University Press, 1984), p. 200.

5. "Howard Florey," n.d., <http://www.abc. net.au/rn/talks/8.30/helthrpt/stories/s12820.htm> (April 12, 2001).

6. Macfarlane, p. 215.

7. Ibid., p. 200.

8. Bullock, p. 103.

9. Maurois, p. 233.

10. Macfarlane, p. 242.

11. Eric G. Anderson, *Medical Economics*, "Here's To the Giants of Medicine," December 20, 1999, p. 64.

Activities

1. "Super-Germ Alert," *Consumer Reports*, January 2001, pp. 60–61.

2. Charles W. Henderson, "Bacteria Becoming Increasingly Resistant to Antibiotics," *World Disease Weekly Plus*, January 25, 1999.

3. Denise Grady, "Drug-Resistant Bacteria Still on the Rise," *The New York Times*, December 28, 2000, p. A21.

4. Walter C. Hellinger, "Confronting the Problem of Increasing Antibiotic Resistance," *Southern Medical Journal*, September 2000, pp. 842–848.

5. Grady, p. A21.

6. "Super-Germ Alert," pp. 60–61.

Glossary

antibiotic—A drug, such as penicillin, that kills bacteria.

antiseptic—Any chemical that kills germs.

bacteria—Tiny living things, also known as microbes, that can cause a variety of diseases.

coccus—Type of bacteria.

germ—Common name for bacteria that cause disease.

lysozyme—A chemical produced by the body that can kill bacteria.

mold—A living thing that often grows on bread and fruit causing them to spoil. Penicillin was first obtained from a mold called *Penicillium*.

penicillin—Chemical that kills certain bacteria.

petri dish—A circular plate with a cover that is filled with nutrients to grow bacteria.

phagocyte—A type of white blood cell that swallows up and destroys bacteria that invade the body.

pneumonia—A disease caused by bacteria that infect the lungs, making breathing difficult.

syphilis—A disease that is transmitted from one person to another through sexual contact and from a mother to her unborn child.

vaccination—The process of giving dead or weakened microbes to protect a person against a particular disease.

Further Reading

Gottfried, Ted. *Alexander Fleming, Discoverer of Penicillin*. New York: Franklin Watts, 1997.

Kaye, Judith. *The Life of Alexander Fleming*. New York: Twenty-First Century Books, 1993.

Otfinoski, Steven. *Alexander Fleming, Conquering Disease with Penicillin*. New York: Facts On File, 1992.

Parker, Steve. *Alexander Fleming*. Chicago: Heinemann Library, 2001.

Tames, Richard. *Alexander Fleming*. Danbury, Conn.: Franklin Watts, 1990.

Internet Addresses

BBC-GCSE Bitesize: Medicine Through Time
http://www.bbc.co.uk/schools/gcsebitesize/history/shp/

Biography of Sir Alexander Fleming
http://nobelprize.org/nobel_prizes/medicine/laureates/1945/fleming-bio.html

TIME 100: Scientists & Thinkers—Alexander Fleming
http://www.time.com/time/time100/scientist/profile/fleming.html

Index